Tipton Poetry Journal
Editor's Note

Tipton Poetry Journal, located in the heart of the Midwest, publishes quality poetry from Indiana and around the world.

Statistics: This issue features 32 poets from the United States (15 different states) and 5 poets from Australia, Bosnia, Canada, and Italy.

Our Featured Poem this issue is "To Mr. Allen, Senior English Teacher, Glen Ridge, New Jersey, a Few Miles from Rutherford, Home of William Carlos Williams," written by Elizabeth Crowell. Elizabeth's poem, which also receives an award of $25, can be found on page 5. The featured poem was chosen by the Board of Directors of Brick Street Poetry, Inc., the Indiana non-profit organization who publishes *Tipton Poetry Journal*.

Barry Harris reviews *My Body the Guitar* by Karla Linn Merrifield.

Dan Carpenter reviews *Catena Poetica: An International Collaboration* by Flor Aguilera, Joyce Brinkman, Gabriele Glang, Carolyn Kreiter-Foronda

Cover Photo: *Wood Ducks at Notre Dame* by Brendan Crowley.

Barry Harris, Editor

Copyright 2022 by the Tipton Poetry Journal.

All rights remain the exclusive property of the individual contributors and may not be used without their permission.

Tipton Poetry Journal is published by Brick Street Poetry Inc., a tax-exempt non-profit organization under IRS Code 501(c)(3). Brick Street Poetry Inc. publishes the Tipton Poetry Journal, hosts the monthly poetry series *Poetry on Brick Street* and sponsors other poetry-related events.

Contents

John Grey 1
Maureen Sherbondy 2
Maria S. Picone 4
Elizabeth Crowell 5
Luanne Castle 6
Anne Whitehouse 7
Karla Linn Merrifield 8
Doris Lynch 9
Tom Raithel 10
Marjie Giffin 12
Claire Scott 13
Jeanine Stevens 17
Victoria Twomey 18
Jennifer L. McClellan 20
VA Smith 22
Jeffrey S. Thompson 24
David Vancil 25
Yuan Changming 26
Duane Anderson 28
Matthew Brennan 28
Ayomide Bayowa 30
Elena Botts 32
Joe Benevento 33
William Greenway 35
Saurabh Sinha 36
Bruce Levine 38
Ian C. Smith 39

Alessio Zanelli	*40*
Jill Evans	*40*
Elya Braden	*42*
Uma Kurt	*44*
Roy Bentley	*44*
Stacy Savage	*46*
Lois Marie Harrod	*47*
Michael Keshigian	*48*
Paul Lojeski	*50*
Review: My Body the Guitar by Karla Linn Merrifield	*51*
Review: Catena Poetica: An International Collaboration	*55*
Contributor Biographies	*60*

A Cure in Winter
John Grey

Just when I'm getting up for living,
it begins to snow again.
Like all winters,
this one never knows when to stop.
The ground is white
and more white falls atop it.
It's like non-living.
No voices.
No music.
Just wind,
that furious nothingness.
And drifts like frozen riptides.
I'm healing
but the outside's come down with something.
It's called weather.
The earth must have caught it from me.

John Grey is an Australian poet, US resident, recently published in the *New World Writing, Dalhousie Review and Blood And Thunder.* Work upcoming in *Hollins Critic, Redactions and California Quarterly.* John lives in Rhode Island.

Skimming Surfaces
Maureen Sherbondy

Lifeguard of tiny creatures
and younger siblings, my brother
floated. Net in hand, he skimmed
the water for sinking flies and spiders.

Ever attentive, later too
he kept watch over me
as I entered high school,
even drawing maps
to guide me through
teenage angst, so I wouldn't
get lost in those noisy hallways.

Now, recalling the kindness
of his ten-year-old self,
I can't come to terms
with the disparate actions
of the man he's become,

how he flattens spiders
beneath his polished
banker's shoes. How now
he only skims those
slick city surfaces
for stocks and gold.

In fact, when I was in need
of rescuing, those dark shoes--
they even stepped on me.

Parosmia

Maureen Sherbondy

At first, I believed it was my dead father's
smoke rising from lungs to tongue,
his three-pack-a-day habit haunting
my body in this post-Covid state.
Weren't you toxic enough while alive?
I whisper to him in the ash-scented air.
But, lo and behold, now I know not
to connect the cause-and-effect
to the chain-smoking deceased.
It's just some bizarre remnant
of the disease. Still, every waking breath
reminds me of Daddy and his refusal
to stay buried in the past.

https://healthcare.utah.edu/healthfeed/postings/2021/09/parosmia.php

https://www.cleveland19.com/2021/12/07/cleveland-woman-suffers-covid-side-effect-that-makes-everything-smell-like-cigarette-smoke/

Maureen Sherbondy has been published in *Calyx, European Judaism, The Oakland Review, Prelude,* and other journals. Her poetry books include *Eulogy for an Imperfect Man, Beyond Fairy Tales, The Art of Departure,* and six chapbooks. *Dancing with Dali* was published by FutureCycle Press in 2020. *Lines in Opposition* will be published by Unsolicited Press in 2022. She has also published a short story collection, *The Slow Vanishing.* Maureen teaches at Alamance Community College and lives in Durham, North Carolina, with her husband Barry Peters and her cat Lola.

Minnesota, late October, 2007
Maria S. Picone

It felt like the beached whale I mourned, salt spleen wind sea birds sea
sick yearning

It felt like a retirement party for summertime ending in Florida
jokes, punctured balloons

It felt like an inside joke when I typed this title, your intimacy
of insults for this New Englander,

It felt like we had sailed to the end of the world & realized it was nothing
but more summers receding, whales beaching, worlds ending—

the belly of it too big, too religious for the mere swallow
of my body, censured from the pass

port of our united states. Starless, star-crossed, we found shore;
we foundered;

to survive, I ate our memories, the way the panes of your cabin shivered,
cracked up under winter's rhythmic skirmishes

& on waking it felt like the branches of my heart stiffened up in the night,
up against this hard frost.

Maria S. Picone/수영 is a Korean American adoptee who won *Cream City Review's* 2020 Summer Poetry Prize. She has been published in *Tahoma Literary Review, The Seventh Wave, Fractured Lit* and more including *Best Small Fictions 2021*. Her work has been supported by *Lighthouse Writers Workshop, GrubStreet, Kenyon Review,* and *Tin House*. She is a 2022 Palm Beach Poetry Festival Kundiman Fellow and Chestnut Review's managing editor. She lives in South Carolina and is also the poetry editor at *Hanok Review* and associate editor at *Uncharted Mag*. Her work explores hybridity, identity, languages, and pop culture. Her website is mariaspicone.com, Twitter @mspicone.

To Mr. Allen, Senior English Teacher, Glen Ridge, New Jersey, a Few Miles from Rutherford, Home of William Carlos Williams

Elizabeth Crowell

One day, he opened the book to the slightest poem
about chickens and a wheelbarrow.
We felt that we did not have much time left.
We could not wait to leave this town.
The trees outside the window were blossoming
on all the corridors of our pretty streets.
He read the poem and asked,
"What is the *so much* that d*epends*?"

I remember looking at
the chicken, the red wheelbarrow,
until I was only staring at the words of them.
That was something, but no way to say it.
The snide boys said it wasn't even a poem
and nothing depends on chicken and rain.

Mr. Allen, with his old leather satchel
on his desk, his jaundiced book laid out
almost like a religious text,
made a sort of face, a "just you wait."
I loved him for this, this sweet man.

My twin brother was one of those boys
and after my mother died,
in a weepy battering rain,
we tried to talk about my father, left behind
without his life-long love of eighty years.
He said, *so much depends*.

Elizabeth Crowell grew up in northern New Jersey and has a B.A. from Smith College in English Literature and an M.F.A. in Creative Writing/Poetry from Columbia University. She taught college and high school English for many years and lives outside of Boston with her wife and teenage children.

Thanks for meeting me for coffee
Luanne Castle

The barista sneaks cynical peeks
at me talking around my tea sips.
She doesn't see you sitting here.
Without your signature hoodie
would she know you from posters?
Every bedtime my mother told me
how you found your grandmother
in the closet and chased off a wolf.
What a brave little girl you were.
I needed to be brave, too, fearing
his sometimes gnashing teeth.
As a teen I learned the huntsman
(merely a hunter after some prey)
saved you; I waited for my own,
mounted and in glinting steel.
I searched for the beginning
of your story and discovered you
were lost when you believed him.
All gone. On a milk carton missing.
Now you're saying that's wrong.
Every version is someone else's story.

Luanne Castle's *Kin Types* (Finishing Line Press), a chapbook of poetry and flash nonfiction, was a finalist for the Eric Hoffer Award. Her first collection of poetry, *Doll God*, winner of the New Mexico-Arizona Book Award for Poetry, was published by Aldrich Press. Luanne has been a Fellow at the Center for Ideas and Society at the University of California, Riverside. She studied English and Creative Writing at the University of California, Riverside (PhD); Western Michigan University (MFA); and Stanford University. Her Pushcart and Best of the Net-nominated poetry and prose have appeared in *Copper Nickel, American Journal of Poetry, Pleiades, River Teeth, TAB, Verse Daily, Glass: A Journal of Poetry, Saranac Review, Grist,* and other journals. An avid blogger, she can be found at luannecastle.com. She lives in Arizona, where she shares land with a bobcat.

Days of 1978
Anne Whitehouse

I remember the bad behavior
of the male professors
in my graduate writing program,
how they preyed on young women,
who were predisposed
to hope their teachers
valued their talents
and would help their careers.

Writing is seduction.
Words have a physical body
that comes to life
when wielded by poets.

When intentions are dishonest,
words become weapons,
and everything gets confused,
emotions running
like rainwater in rivulets
trying to find a course
or make one.

Anne Whitehouse's recent poetry collection is *Outside from the Inside* (Dos Madres Press, 2020), and her recent chapbook is *Escaping Lee Miller* (Ethel Zine and Micro Press, 2021).. Anne is also the author of a novel, *Fall Love,* and she has been publishing a series of essays about Edgar Allan Poe. She lives in New York City and Columbia County, New York. www.annewhitehouse.com

As My Husband Lies Dying
Karla Linn Merrifield

*Conscience is our guide, whatever trappings
we might choose to clothe it in.*
                    ~~Noam Chomsky

Daydreaming has become a lost art.
Poetry is dead.
My imagination gasps to escape.

Vivid images à la viciousness like viper-pit venom
dripping down an IV line into my mind.
Vacuity: On the Matthias YouTube Channel,

one of ten strange dollar-store items sent
by viewers— tiny scented hot-sauce, taco,
and tostada erasers for poor kids to choke on.

I'm trapped in the whack-job's meme machine.
Weather.com is calling for violent tweetstorms.
Lies. Lies. Lies. Lies. Lies. Lies. Lies. Lies.

But then I turn my eyes to night's summer sky,
view fully the full Thunder Moon, my bright light.

Karla Linn Merrifield has had 1000+ poems appear in dozens of journals and anthologies. She has 14 books to her credit. Following her 2018 *Psyche's Scroll* (Poetry Box Select) is the 2019 full-length book *Athabaskan Fractal: Poems of the Far North* from Cirque Press. Her newest poetry collection, *My Body the Guitar*, inspired by famous guitarists and their guitars, was published in December 2021 by Before Your Quiet Eyes Publications Holograph Series (Rochester, NY). Karla now lives in Florida.

In the Hours Between Midnight and Morning
Doris Lynch

We escape our souls, even our bodies.
In the ebony hours, we ferry meteors
tiny as rice grains up the alabaster
mountains that in daylight we call clouds.
Our child-sized buckets jingle whenever
they accidentally touch.

Transformed by the power of dreams
we wander in the wee hours
above the earth, our nightgowns
and PJs swishing, slippers loosening
nodules of frozen rain, while
a hundred million xylophones
form a space backup band.

Sounds that intelligent beings on another
planet might label static or, more hopefully,
music. But when we arrive on this sister planet,
instead of offering its denizens
fiery trinkets or buckets silvery as stars,
we stand, mouths agape, unable to sing
in any tongue beyond our own.

Doris Lynch has recent work in *Flying Island, Failed Haiku, Contemporary Haibun Online,* and *Drifting Sands Haibun.* She has lived in places as varied as arctic Alaska, Yogyakarta, Indonesia, New Orleans, Berkeley, and for the last twenty-some years in Bloomington, Indiana.

The Readers
Tom Raithel

At tables and desks, surrounded by bookshelves,
they bend to their screens and pages,
silently drinking words with their eyes.

Rainbowed coronas swell around their heads,
and inside each— a separate world.
Here, a physicist chalks an equation.

There, a birdwatcher catalogs sparrows.
Now the conductor finds blood on luggage
as the train steams through Siberian night.

Though thunder outside resounds through the library,
readers stay fixed to their spheres
until one closes her book with a thud,

bursting her cloud. Its residue falls.
When she walks out to the rain-soaked street,
rainbow dust still clings to her eyes.

Children of the Wind
Tom Raithel

They love to hide, but you hear their whispers
as they run through grass or climb into trees.

They'll topple a yard sign, knock off a hat,
or scatter a neighbor's leaves through your yard.

Bored and ignored by grown-ups before,
and lured by a sense of adventure,

they stepped out one day into open air,
and the air took them in. Spirits now,

they're not afraid of the dark anymore.
They won't come in when called.

On bad days, though, you hear them cry,
mourning their loss of embraceable form.

Then they may rush up to you on your walk
and hug you with gusty arms.

Tom Raithel grew up in Milwaukee, Wisconsin and has worked as a journalist at several newspapers in the Midwest. Recently from Evansville, Indiana, today, he lives in Cleveland, Ohio with his wife, Theresa. His poems have appeared in *The Southern Review, The Comstock Review, Nimrod, Midwest Quarterly, Atlanta Review*, and other journals. Finishing Line Press has published his chapbook, *Dark Leaves, Strange Light*.

Cardiologist
Marjie Giffin

I guessed my pressures might rise the second
I crossed the threshold into your room,
a space where the slightest fluctuations
are duly captured and transmitted

on undulating screens that strain my neck
to read and can only be caught in waves
that I ride with eyes and stomach juices
churning as I squint across an airless divide.

Why am I afraid? The heart doesn't lie.
Mine will not betray me, but it might reveal
secrets of its own that I prefer not to know
as I lie here chilled, draped in scanty gown.

Cold and sticky tabs dot my chest and relay
graphic messages that spell out my fate:
Is my inner clock ticking to a healthy beat
or is it time to trade for a new mechanism

to keep me vital, to keep me free
of tethers to meds and breathing tanks
and pitying glances and weekly trips
to see you, the one I dread, cardiologist?

Marjie Giffin is a Midwestern writer who has authored four regional histories and whose poetry has appeared in *Snapdragon, Poetry Quarterly, Flying Island, The Kurt Vonnegut Literary Journal, Saint Katherine Review, Northwest Indiana Literary Journal, Blue Heron Review, Tipton Poetry Journal, Agape Review* and the anthologies *The Lives We Have Live(d)* and *What Was and What Will Be, Leave them Something,* and *Reflections on Little Eagle Creek.* Her work was recently featured online by the Heartland Society of Women Writers and her first chapbook, *Touring,* was published in 2021. She lives in Indianapolis and is active in the Indiana Writers' Center and has taught both college writing and gifted education.

Off Balance
Claire Scott

When did the balance shift
like a playground seesaw
or a emptying hourglass.
When did it shift from looking
forward to my grandchild's graduation
or a sun-soaked cruise in the Greek islands
to looking back, trolling for memories
of a temple in Erice or maybe Segesta,
of winning the school spelling bee
with the word *reminiscence*
or was that my sister?
How did I not notice?

Serried memories blur, overlap, dim and disappear.
I make my wobbled way to the sofa and
page through old albums, photos taken
centuries before cell phones, some with black
triangles in the corners, gluing them in place.
Who are all these people looking
like life is a lark, a walk in a tree-lined park?
Could that be Aunt Jennie or possibly cousin Rachel
who died last year of diabetes or dementia or despair?
Didn't they know most people die?
That we are all riding a roller coaster on the way
down, holding onto life with a death grip.

Why not close the albums, bundle up
and step outside even if your legs are unsteady, even
if your fingers are freezing and winter seems
reluctant to leave, its unrelenting rawness
seeping your bones. Feel the soft sting of snowflakes
on your tongue, listen to the call of tree sparrows.
If you are lucky, you will loosen your grip,
enjoy the giddy ride, the glistening trees,
the giggling children, the Sunday farmers
selling Brussels sprouts and kale.
If you are lucky, you will wake to a spring
that still includes you.

Variations on the Theme of Hope
Claire Scott

Grinning emojis, emailed clichés
        hope the party is fun, hope it won't
                rain, hope you sleep well
balloons ripple across our screens
        we groan and delete

Cynicism is winning ladies and gentlemen
        odds are on Sixth Extinction
                favored ten to one over Bright Morning
we cheer for Morning's hammering hooves
        as we guzzle fossil fuels
                gobble steaks and burgers
                        vote *no* on affordable housing

While writing checks to the Sierra Club
        putting social justice signs on our lawns
                Kindness is Everything
enjoying the hit of hope
        like a needle slipped into our veins
                knowing full well it is too late

Perhaps we should go back and back
        to where we first left hope behind

The moment the doctor said *I'm so sorry*
        and looked down at her iPad
the second our boyfriend
        furled his fist
to just before a child
        runs into the street
                chasing her red and blue soccer ball

We might find Hope cowering in the weeds
        by the side of a six lane highway
                soaked and shivering
or perhaps in the bottom of a sealed jar
        barely able to breathe
        the only god left

Don't open it some people warn

      stay in the present
      breathe from your Hara

Hope leads to craving and serious suffering
      splitting time into today and tomorrow
            when there is only *now*

Others believe there is room
      for a hope that includes all beings
           like a prayer
           from the center of the earth

Try settling Hope on the green cushion by the fire
      feed her like a little bird and play
           wordless tunes on a lyre,

Until the weather shifts
      and she is ready to lift again
           wearing a cape of white feathers

No Serotonin Left
Claire Scott

Help! My serotonin is reuptaking
by the gigatonne. Neurons
greedily slurping like a black Lab
licking ice cream on the sidewalk
outside Baskin-Robbins.

Little left to carry upbeat messages
around my brain in brown leather
satchels or JanSport backpacks. Memories
of Santa Claus, shiny quarters from
my uncle or Max making mischief.

More like Red Riding Hood with an empty
basket or the Easter Bunny with no tinted eggs.
I lie in bed like an ancient grandmother with
a white kerchief around her head. The wolves
of depression knocking at the door.

Claire Scott is an award winning poet in Oakland, California who has received multiple Pushcart Prize nominations. Her work has been accepted by the *Atlanta Review, Bellevue Literary Review, New Ohio Review, Enizagam* and *Healing Muse* among others. Claire is the author of *Waiting to be Called* and *Until I Couldn't*. She is the co-author of *Unfolding in Light: A Sisters' Journey in Photography and Poetry*.

Sunchokes
Jeanine Stevens

Let summer burst to wholeness
the rind and husk stand firm.

Let olives fatten black and oily
on Van Gogh's gnarled branches.

May the female dragonfly, in a dither
recognize the male's transformation

from deep turquoise to glistening copper
to match the drying earth.

Let us notice Red Cloud's blue moon above
smoke filled tamaracks and call it lovely.

In record heat, roadways buckle and heave,
tar breaks into chunks like fudge.

Rivers change course, new villages spring up
and folks revise old kinship charts.

No going back to past epochs, the romance
of the three-toed camel, the albino musk ox.

Now, a more reasonable garden of chiggers
and sunchokes all recreated by the same God.

Jeanine Stevens is the author of *Inheritor and Limberlost* (Future Cycle Press), and *Sailing on Milkweed* (Cherry Grove Collections). She is winner of the MacGuffin Poet Hunt and The Ekphrasis Prize. Gertrude Sitting: Portraits of Women, won the 2020 Chapbook Prize from Heartland Review Press. Jeanine recently received her seventh Pushcart Nomination. She studied poetry at U.C. Davis and Community of Writers, Olympic Valley and is Faculty Emerita at American River College.

Neither Kindness nor Cruelty
Victoria Twomey

though the man was sure
he had taught her a lesson
she would never forget
with the orderly cut
of his sharp metal plough

the Wild, in no hurry
laughed as she kept time
with her flying dandelion clocks
her circling hawks
her loyal following of shadows

she was a being
he did not understand
who spoke
with doppler'd wing songs
slimy croaking toads
one-note owls

she was a self-sufficient metamorphic
who understood
the history of the wind
what it might bring
what it might take away

having axed his chickens
fenced his cows
mastered his porch-dwelling dog
and the horse that pulled his plough
the man was sure
he could command her to follow
his seasons of need

she was patient with his folly
knowing someday
with her slow and inevitable entanglements
her clever raccoons
her hungry moles and rabbits
her legions of stem borers
pod suckers, aphids and weevils
she would reclaim his ordered field

with neither kindness
nor cruelty
with the help of the sun and rain
she knew she would pull down his barn
and give it to the bats and spiders
then bring his plough to its broken, rusted knees

in time
when his widow buried him beneath a tree
and made an offering of his body
the Wild gathered him in
embraced him with her encircling roots
loved him
deeply
until they were one

Victoria Twomey is a fine art illustrator and the author of several chapbooks, including *Autumn Music Box* and *The Feminine Voice*. She has appeared as a featured poet at various venues around Long Island including "First Fridays" at the Hecksher Museum of Art, The Poetry Barn, Barnes & Noble, The Pisces Cafe, Borders Books and local radio. Her poems have been published in several anthologies, in newspapers and on the Web. Her poem "Pieta" was nominated for a Pushcart Prize by *Long Island Sounds 2006: An Anthology of Poetry From Maspeth to Montauk and Beyond*.

Changing Hands
Jennifer L. McClellan

I'm standing
on the retrospective isthmus
that connects
two divergent parts of myself;
who I am with you
who I'll be without you.

The part of me
I recognize has a hand that reaches
over the end table,
careful not to tip sideways
the vase of honeysuckle and coral roses,
as I gently squeeze your hand
like you've always done to mine
when I've needed reassurance.
I bought you a yellow summer shirt
in case you decide to step outside
to watch the birds at the feeders,
but as of late you only go
where I push you in your wheelchair
and this morning has been still
in the living room, your arthritic hands
no longer able to do needlework.
The light filters through the sheer white
curtains as we listen to Andy Williams'
lustrous voice sing "May Each Day"
and my throat tightens.

I watch the ageless golden couple, ceaselessly
revolve under the glass domed anniversary clock.
They spin with a weightlessness I envy.
An unawareness of the inevitable things
that have found us: a hefty medicine schedule,
oxygen tubes, nurse home visits,
and the weight of your body leaning
on my shoulders as I help you get dressed.
Dad's been gone twelve and a half years,
but at least his picture is still on the mantle place.
I wish I could watch the two of you dance again.
I wish you and I could dance again, painlessly,
like the tiny couple keeping time
to this old song you know the words to.

The part of me I recognize
still has you and your mind is there
and knows who I am: your sixth son
always trying to keep a smile on your face.
Your smile is the strongest part of your body
and just briefly makes me feel like you're young
and happy again.
Then the timer buzzes for me to remove
the ice packs from your hips
and I hope your pain has lessened.
This is the part I don't recognize.

Jennifer L. McClellan is an Evansville, Indiana based poet whose poems have been published in the *Tipton Poetry Journal, Flying Island, Stirring: A Literary Collection, The Green Hills Literacy Lantern* as well as an upcoming issue of *The The Round Table Literary Journal*.

To Be Zorro
VA Smith

Child of a prefab ranch house,
of a *Woman's Day* mom, I lacked,
at 7, intimacy with the gothic,
though I still knew that
a lonely Victorian on a hill
facing a cemetery was
out of my league.

What landed me here, in part,
was my ministry to grade school
outcasts, bound to bring them to
the safe center
where taunts about being poor, smelly,
an eater of nose matter, wearer
of torn clothes might end.

Stevie Jones was such a rescue.
More than that, small, quiet, brainy,
he was, by some as yet invisible
metric, a boy from the right kind
of people, my mother declared:
shabby genteel Southerners
transplanted to our hard scrabble
town, where his grandmother and mine
played bridge, garden clubbed, attended
Episcopal Trinity together,
recalcitrant ladies among
the bubbas.

So there I stood on All Hallow's Eve,
as Stevie's librarian mother
called it, ready for Trick or Treat.
Though I'd declined candy cream pumpkins
collecting cat hair on Stevie's
bedside table, I worked my pony-tailed
best at bounciness, looking eager
to fill my sack with sugary bribes.
Into the night we went, good girl turned
wicked witch, gentle boy aching
to be Zorro.

Heading home, bags bulging with sweets,
I felt the pirates on us
from behind, wrestling the booty
from our grip as I kicked, scratched and bit,
Stevie brandishing his sword only
to see it splintered over the knee
of one big kid, the second pushing
me to the ground while grabbing the spoils,
both hag and hero scrapped, bloody, scared.
After they'd left I scrambled to find
the hats, hand the gaucho bowler
to Zorro, search the dry leaves for
my black felt conical, flattened
and torn.
  . . . . .

In high school we're still secret friends.
He carries me through Chemistry,
I curate his clothes and hair.
Graduation night, I come in
Magna to his Summa, later
get him high in his neighborhood
graveyard, where, stoned dramatic,
we swear we will trade hats,
Crone to Folk Hero, and back,
all our lives.

VA Smith lives in Philadelphia and has published poetry in dozens of literary journals and anthologies, among them *Blue Lake Review, Ginosko Literary Journal, MacQueen's Quinterly, Mobius, Quartet, The Southern Review, Verdad, Third Wednesday, Oyster River Pages*, and forthcoming in *Evening Street Review* and *West Trade Review*, Her book *Biking Through the Stone Age* will be published by Kelsay Books in Spring 2022. Currently, she's finishing a collection titled *America's Daughters & Other Poems* and ignoring her Peleton.

Late Winter

Jeffrey S. Thompson

My tail was still wagging
When the universe said
I'll give you something
To worry about.

Swings swing
In the empty playground
While a toddler-sized crow
Patrols the sidewalks.

Houses left half-
Empty, shuddering
Against the wind,
Surround the cemetery

Where I laid out
My hangover
And my ruined shoes.
The Black Angel

Points to the Hilltop.
A sheet of newspaper
Or a stray terrier
Bounds across the dirty snow.

Jeffrey S. Thompson was raised in Fargo, North Dakota, and educated at the University of Iowa and Cornell Law School. He lives and works in Phoenix, Arizona. At Iowa he participated in undergraduate poetry workshops and had a couple poems published in small journals. He pursued a career in public interest law, but recently decided to start sharing his work again. Thompson was named a finalist for the 2021 *Iowa Review Poetry* Award, and has been published or accepted at *Neologism Poetry Journal, North Dakota Quarterly, The Main Street Rag,* and *Passengers Journal.*

The Captain Who Wouldn't Fight
David Vancil

He was slick looking, a graduate of college and OCS.
He had a CIB, which means he'd seen some shit.
The brass had sent him to stay with us until he rotated,
two weeks to be coddled. "He's done his part,"
we'd been told. "Treat him with proper respect."

The first thing he did was tell us the war was bad—
we had no reason to be in disagreement, showing
we understood. "Then why are you fighting?"
he demanded. "Why don't you tell them you quit."

None of us said a thing. What could we reply?
"We're following orders until we can't or die."

He was someone with spine, someone who knew
what we wouldn't admit to. Yet, when we saw him
coming, we stepped aside. He made us uneasy.
He had too many questions and was much too certain.

When he departed, we wished him well. We stood by
and shook his hand. No one spoke his name again.

David Vancil is retired from the faculty of Indiana State University. His work has appeared in small periodicals, critical reviews, and a few anthologies. As well, he is the author of four poetry collections. *War and Its Discontents*, a collection of military poems centered on family service and his own time in the U.S. Army, will be published by Angelina River Press sometime in 2022. He is at work on a collection of new and selected poems, which he hopes to publish no later than 2023. David lives in Terre Haute, Indiana, with his wife, three cats, and a dog.

Mindful Mindset
Yuan Changming

1/ Here: Into the Reality

You see, here's the leaf dyed with the full
Spectrum of autumn; here's the dewdrop
Containing all the dreams made on the
Darkest corner of last night; here's the
Light pole in the forest where gods land
From another higher world; here's the swirl
You can dance with to release all your
Stresses against the Virus. Here you are in
Deed as in need embracing
The most
Mindful moment, when you can readily
Measure your feel with each breath, but do
Not think about time, which is nothing but
A pure human invention. Just point every
Synapse of yours to this locale. *Here* is *now*

2/ Now: The Art of Living

   With my third eye I glaze into
The present moment, & there I find it
Full of pixels, each of which is
Unfurling slowly like a koru into
A whole new brave world that I
Can spend days, even months to watch
As if from
       A magic kaleidoscope

Dusk Walk: for Helena Qi Hong
Yuan Changming

Taking a walk around the neighborhood at sunset

Leaves rustling as if crows have just flapped by

In the twilight sky, the moon looms-

What if such loomings vanish into an unknown space
As clouds exchange their feels in a hurry?

Seeing a passer-by coming my way, I derailed my body & thought alike

What if the planet really comes to a pause during the Pandemic?
What if social distancing becomes the order of the day for ever?
What if the season, in other words, lasts between rain and snow?

Seeing two teenagers approaching, I jumped aside and hip-hoped
On the curb edge like a lousy dancer as they ran along

What if the doors of my homeland remain close until I am too
Old or too week to move to see & kiss my first & last love?

What if my family cannot afford to immigrate to Mars from this burning
Or frozen planet? What if another huge meteorite hits earth hard enough?

Seeing a dog-walker come up, I quicken my steps and turn
To an empty sidewalk, smelling marijuana like dog's fart

What if what I know is neither true nor false if
Thought against reality?

Yuan Changming hails with Allen Yuan from poetrypacific.blogspot.ca. Credits include 12 Pushcart nominations & chapbooks (most recently *Limerence*) besides appearances in *Best of the Best Canadian Poetry* (2008-17) & *Best New Poems Online*, among more than 1900 others. Yuan served on the jury, and was nominated, for Canada's National Magazine Awards (poetry category) and lives in Vancouver.

Frozen Watering Hole
Duane Anderson

The birdbath was
closed for the season
with winter's arrival,
the water in the bowl, now frozen.

Skate rentals were unavailable
though birds came anyway
doing spins and spirals
as they slid across the ice.

A watering hole,
one that no longer
quenched one's thirst.
An oasis, closed until spring.

Duane Anderson currently lives in La Vista, Nebraska, and volunteers with a non-profit organization as a Donor Ambassador on their blood drives. He has had poems published in *The Pangolin Review, Fine Lines, The Sea Letter, Cholla Needles, Tipton Poetry Journal, Adelaide Literary Magazine* and several other publications.

Scatman Crothers of Terre Haute Stars in *The Shining*
Matthew Brennan

Some places shine, the hotel chef explained,
and some just don't. When Scatman was a teen,
the city shined: dark nights and early mornings,
he fingered frets and kept the beat on snares
in speakeasies north of Sycamore and in
the alley next to Hulman's Dry Goods Store.

He took this jivin' shine on tour to Harlem,
then the bright lights of Vegas. Next, LA
enticed him; money flowed for Jim Crow roles:
caretaker, corpse, a liveryman and bellhop,
shoeshine boy, barker at a carnival.
His wick went out. He felt he'd lost the beat.

But then he brought to life the hotel chef
in Kubrick's film *The Shining*, one who sensed
the living past of The Overlook Resort:
the swinging jazz and clinking gin and tonics
on summer nights, the bloody bad times too,
visions he'd wake from late while deep in sleep.

Like the young Scatman home in Terre Haute
watching with his grandma from her porch
the winter skies beyond the railroad tracks—
both seeing more than they can say—the chef
could feel the future when a blizzard buried
and closed the roads in Colorado, saw

into the center of all shapes, his highbeams
hewing a path through blinding snow-packed darkness.

Matthew Brennan's poems have appeared in *Poetry Salzburg, Concho River Review, Valparaiso Poetry Review, THINK, Paterson Literary Review, Tipton Poetry Journal,* and others. His most recent book is *Snow in New York: New and Selected Poems* (2021). He taught for 32 years at Indiana State University and now lives in Columbus, Ohio.

Speculum
Ayomide Bayowa

I offered an empty grace palm on a Sunday sermon
prayer with an open eye. My mother nodded away a
lizard dance & her pious dough, just as she'd to my
immediate father's cracked mirror, all day and night—
the way she already shoved the satisfaction box of
every man.

As learnt— that which chases a woman from a man
to another: asylum not *strumpetry*— the same drive
for new church members. Rough-handed givers,
hardening their faiths on their Naira notes,
burdening the ushers with after-service palm
straightening monotony.

Heavens straightened whenever a young man
became her sanctuary. She whistled my head, a
kettle placed to her hot chest and chanted in
five tongues— one of which is a quick nuptial
layout.
That was how I was birthed: '...*from stutters to the littlest of chance given to a stranger.*'
The long-heard first words that brought light into her blindfolded heart.

She wore a tall cerulean miniskirt— tall and lined as our
front room's curtain. Or short as her thigh flesh,
herding the doddery of a just found *age-is-mere-number*
sheep in a famine field.

Every time she thought the color of my eyes was her
rose's first choice, things started to tear: the Leukemia
clouds losing their cotton in drifting wools, as I chased to
catch up her moving boat in a fragment question of that
which claimed to have come through the backdoor in
peace and to stay— with a booster bag and barrel-shaped
forehead.

For months, I sat outside, a jilted figure under our home's
number sign, with eyes vase(d)— like a water container well-
positioned under the gutter to collect the evening rains.
Everyone passing by had flooding questions about my
mother's whereabout(s)— until now, that I am a stink-face
dancer. Shaking my legs behind a familiar refugee camp tent,
the only dance I can think of, after a regional clinic's male
nurse says my prolapsed womb is an upshot of my one too
many swears at science.

& It could be called *'bata,'* the fast-paced move of
the *Yorubas*: that speak dust, barefooted. The
lightning god's drummers understand what I
mean— What it is like to be struck and dumped
behind a third shelter where survivors' prayers are
bruise flames on lips— quick sucks to make idolatry
sounds, should you catch a sight
of yourself in the mirror. Fear kicking at and from
the gut of the gut, spitting saliva to extinguish a
cooking protest, in the blurriness of eyes I should
have left underneath our house's number sign.

& With my skin flaying from the smile of an
eclipse to my shadow, with a truth tied up with an
old scarf like market women's tattered cash,
I hack the air with feathery worship— blessing my body for this rite
I've for so-long neglected: "...finding the unknown in roman numerals of dry bones
& Rhetorical questions: swollen bellies, earth caesarean, earth caesarean."

Ayomide Bayowa is the (2021-24) poet laureate of Mississauga, Ontario, Canada. He became the first place in the 2020 July Open Drawer Poetry Contest, the June/ July 2021 Edition of the Bi-monthly Brigitte Poirson Poetry Contest (BPPC). He was a top-ten gold entrant of the 9th Open Eurasian Literary Festival, U.K, and a semi-finalist of the 2021 Cave Canem Poetry Prize. He has appeared in a long list of literary magazines, some of which are *Barren Magazine, Agbowó, Guesthouse-Lit, Stone of Madness Press*. He currently reads poetry for *Adroit Journal*.

this time I give you a rose
Elena Botts

yes, i long for you
there is no doubt in my mind,
in my mind there is no doubt
in my mind

we are all so soon to die
have so little time
to lie in bed with the radio on
to check the post for the relative gone
to wear the pink skirt and the embroidered top
with jewel earrings.

i will try to determine what it is in your bright dark eyes
what it is you are made of
like some dear sister or brother
my spine to your spine
the separation this kiss implies
i am yours to find

in this wide forever night
to render the winter peace
with the thoughtlessness of landscape in deep sleep
a deer with one antler torn wanders
the lost clearing i imagine you
come anew, pure and so true
knowing what it is. you are one thing

and i am another, spoken out loud
differing in my pulse and mind,
feeling intemperate beside you,
knowing i am torn from you by the message i have left
of sincere appreciation
this devotion makes me, and takes me north along the road

in the language of an earth we will age out of
and in the bliss of unknowing, fall out and in again
to the beauteous oblivion,
this time i give you a rose.
adorn your cheek, if you like
with this or some other symbol
to take with you
along the way

i will bless you beyond whichever grave
of water, this or that river,
for you, as in death, i will reconsider
the word "love".

Elena Botts has lived many places in the northeast and abroad, currently in New York state. Her poems have been published in over a hundred literary magazines, and she is the winner of four poetry contests and has had many books published. Her visual artwork has won numerous awards and has been exhibited in various galleries. Elena has also collaborated on, released and installed sound and moving image artwork, as well as multimedia and conceptual art, and formed a multimedia collective for this purpose, while pursuing graduate school, human rights, and arts projects.

A-Fib and the Fly
Joe Benevento

"I heard a Fly buzz-when I died" - Emily Dickinson

Two-fifty AM and my first arrhythmia in nine months.

I've had this condition since before I was fifty, but back then
the doctors said, after my cardiac catheterization showed
how wide my arteries were, I had little to worry about,
particularly since I always settled back to sinus rhythm.

Now, though, experts inside my treacherous television exclaim
even five minutes of atrial fibrillation greatly increases
the chance for a stroke, so instead of sleeping through
this bout, I stay awake waiting for the numbness,
the tingling towards the potential panicked call
to the ER.

I go off to the bathroom further from where my wife sleeps
so as not to awaken or worry her.
As I sit contemplating my mortality from the toilet seat
I consider all the ironies: a friend not ten hours earlier
telling me about an acquaintance younger than us who died
in her sleep during a trip to Acapulco;
the line I used when the cleaning woman at work remarked
on all the people my age who had retired recently: "Yeah,
they're dropping like flies, but I'm going to try flying a little longer."

This line buzzes most in my brain because of my company:
a fly no happier than I to be awake and feeling trapped inside.
My instinct is to get up to try to swat him, but I get the idea
someone this close to death or debilitation should consider
letting live all other life.

Still, the fly keeps buzzing me, so I do get up, pull my pajama pants
back to go mode, grab a hand towel, and, surprising to us both,
soon have him crushed and in the wastebasket, a black dot in a field
of used white tissues.

In the end, no matter the final outcome awaiting me,
I have chosen to be ruthless,
like life is.

Joe Benevento's poems, stories, essays and reviews have appeared in close to 300 places, including: *Poets & Writers, I-70 Review* and *Bilingual Review*. He is the author of fourteen books of poetry and fiction, including: *Expecting Songbirds: Selected Poems, 1983-2015*. He teaches creative writing and American literature at Truman State University in Kirksville, Missouri. and is the poetry editor for the *Green Hills Literary Lantern*.

Fossils

William Greenway

I try to get my daughter to take
one of my books to show and tell,
a proud moment
I've always dreamed of,
but she rolls her eyes in her new
give-me-a-break sign-language
and takes instead another
stuffed animal.

Or at least take the two ammonites
we bought in Lyme Regis, the snail
shells curled and ribbed
like fetal vertebrae still here,
the flesh gone.

Or the block of salt the student gave me,
the size of a Mars bar but almost transparent
after three million years at the bottom
of Lake Erie.

But fossils to her are just more rocks,
and what's a million years, much less three
to a young girl with a boyfriend already
in the 2nd grade, who, she knows,
knows everything, and will never be as old
as her old man.

And, after all, she's right:
a poem really is nothing,
just another shell,
the flesh gone.

William Greenway's 13th collection, As Long As We're Here, is forthcoming from FutureCycle Press. His *Selected Poems* was the Poetry Book of the Year Award winner from FutureCycle Press, and his tenth collection, *Everywhere at Once,* won the Poetry Book of the Year Award from the Ohio Library Association, as did his eighth collection *Ascending Order*. Publications include *Poetry, American Poetry Review, Southern Review, Missouri Review, Georgia Review, Southern Poetry Review, Prairie Schooner, Poetry Northwest,* and *Shenandoah.* Greenway is Distinguished Professor of English Emeritus at Youngstown State University, and now lives in Ephrata, Pennsylvania.

Regarding the third of three consecutive teenagers in a trauma bay who were fatally shot within one week in West Philadelphia during the summer of 2019

Saurabh Sinha

I.

they shot me today mama i ain't do nothin i sweartoyou it's not how you raised me to get shot like that. i think it's gonna hurt you more than it hurt me mama i ain't even know nothin happened. really. i was just walkin by myself and that was that the end i guess. maybe if i talked a little more and had some friends with me i wouldn'ta been alone you always said i should talk more din't you? that i was shy or that i was too quiet like or i need to stand up for myself? well anyway listen mama i don't got much time but no one gonna tell you the real story. the doctors cut open my chest i'm glad you didn't see mama but then they said it was too late too. they'll call you mama someone gonna call you. they'll tell you some things but no one gonna know that i was just walkin mama. i was thinkin about how i wanted to get back home and that i was tired and some other stuff i can't remember now but it was all small things really. anyway so when they call you mama, just know i ain't do nothin wrong. maybe some things but nothin big was all small things. make sure you breathe too mama when they call you, like you taught me in and out when i got nervous

II.

On a CT scan, bright are:
blood, bone,
      & bullet fragments.

Darker are infarcted, lifeless
basal ganglia, brainstem,
& the momentary vacuum of a trauma bay
seconds after
      "Time of Death: 12:01".

III.

fr what.
FR WHAT!
my
      baby.

them curls is his yes –

he ain't do nothin!

     my
           tormnt.

may,

may i nevr sleep again 4 chnce to
     hear   his

                             whisper;

Saurabh Sinha is a neurosurgery resident based in Philadelphia, PA. His poetry focuses on his everyday life, ranging from profound moments with his patients, to the shared journey of early parenthood with his wife, to simply walking his dog.

The First Snowfall of Winter
Bruce Levine

The first snowfall of winter
Singular crystals of water
floating on currents of air
Drifting through time and space
A syllogism drawn on frosted car windows
Green grass turned white
to crackle under feet while walking dogs
Footprints outlining the path
A new beginning shaping itself
into a new reality
Focusing on visions culled from dreams
Creating an environment
tangible to the eye and the senses
Longed for realities realized
as the first snowfall of winter
Drifts across the landscape
permeating the conscious and subconscious
Cutting and pasting happy times
into a scrapbook in the heart
The first snowfall of winter
Paper white and crystal clear
Covering the earth and blanketing the soul

Bruce Levine has spent his life as a writer of fiction and poetry and as a music and theatre professional. A 2019 *Pushcart Prize* Poetry nominee, a 2021 *Spillwords Press Awards* winner, the *Featured Writer* in WestWard Quarterly Summer 2021 and his bio is featured in *"Who's Who of Emerging Writers 2020."* Bruce has over three hundred works published on over twenty-five on-line journals including *Ariel Chart, Spillwords, The Drabble*; in over seventy print books including *Poetry Quarterly, Haiku Journal, Tipton Poetry Journal; Halcyon Days* and *Founder's Favourites* (on-line and print) and his shows have been produced in New York and around the country. His work is dedicated to the loving memory of his late wife, Lydia Franklin. A native Manhattanite, Bruce now lives and writes in Maine. Visit him at www.brucelevine.com

Gridlocked

Ian C. Smith

Immersing old aches in my steaming bath solving a giant crossword, I come across JFK and his PT boat, jacquescousteau plunging down, down, even a coracle, and a water-filled ditch surrounding a castle, but no sign of Shelley among fathomable opportunities. A lake in Whitman's *Passage to India*? Tahoe seems more film noir.

I ignore my phone interrupting the affirmative Molly Bloom, like clues about writers, artists, characters, trying not to waterlog them. The Brontes are here, my glasses becoming a Haworth of fog. Scipio struts in from 202 BC, and I don't flag, filling in an Aussie actor originally a comedian. Don Quixote is simple. Auden, Diaghilev, and Sylvia Plath, appear, then James Dean in the appropriate sized puzzle. Good old Vladimir and Estragon move me along, oddly. Bedevilled by dodgy memory, I am also abetted by Faust.

A clue about a mystery musicologist, moniker Ebenezer, drifts thoughts towards Christmas, and wonderfully obsolete names. Filling in *Bolero* its earworm threatens to unravel me. Soaring around the world in eighty minutes, Europa leads to Zagreb, but African capitals are a weakness. One tricky answer, extramural, could describe me. I almost splash the page again when Charybdis fits after I flounder, all at sea, brain whirling dizzyingly.

Like life, crossword difficulty eases somewhat towards the end, but is tough to complete. I know nothing about pinball machines, religious jurisdictions, or leaders of the Helvetians, stubborn unanswerables spelling failure. I biro in Femme fatale?'s answer, Bette Davis spot on about old age being no place for sissies. Were she alive, she would probably rasp a ready witticism about becoming a puzzle answer. *Requiem* seems a fitting end. Well, it's your funeral, Mozart, I think, skin wrinkling. It was to begin with. If I am not cheating.

Ian C. Smith's work has been published in *Antipodes, BBC Radio 4 Sounds, The Dalhousie Review, Griffith Review, San Pedro River Review , Southword, The Stony Thursday Book, & Two Thirds North*. His seventh book is *wonder sadness madness joy*, Ginninderra (Port Adelaide). He writes in the Gippsland Lakes area of Victoria, Australia and on Flinders Island.

A Walk at Dusk
Alessio Zanelli

Some say the twilight's best
enjoyed by rocking on
the porch. Until it's dark.
I think it is no time
to rest. Its hues can be
much brighter than the day's.
Then who recalls the dawn's?
I'm going to shake off
the blues, put on my shoes,
step out towards the west
and meet the setting sun.
I'm in no rush, and yet
I have to mind each pace.
The dusk, you know, that's earned.

Alessio Zanelli is an Italian poet who writes in English and whose work has appeared in over 200 literary journals from 16 countries. His fifth original collection, titled *The Secret Of Archery*, was published in 2019 by Greenwich Exchange Publishing (London). For more information please visit www.alessiozanelli.it.

Turning the Corner
Jill Evans

I thought I saw your shadow
as you turned the corner of our house.
You loped long-legged like a boy,
your arms, the ones I know by heart,
all tangled up in fallen tree limbs
after last night's storm.

You were on a mission
so you didn't feel time's pinhole
cling to your elusive light,
like me, memorizing you
from our wooden deck.

I thought this
well might be my dream

of you, walking, busy and blurred
and too swiftly out of sight
around the corner of our house.

Your hands were brimming
with brown bags and muddy trowels,
your knees sweat green from kneeling
on soggy springtime grass. Head full
of jumbled tasks
still left to do. You left no wet footprints

stretching backward
as you moved on ahead.
You were really there – and here,

in this timeless present-tense
of our emerging everydays. Planting grasses,
dumping trash, thinking of a beer.
How do I prolong

the undamaged here and now of you
when a shadow
of our future hovers
just around an aging turn
of our blooming garden?

Jill Evans, aka: Jill Evans Petzall, makes documentary films, media art installations, writes poetry, and teaches about social justice from a female perspective. She lives in St. Louis, Missouri. Her work is fueled by a graduate degree in Philosophy and her faith in the power of storytelling. She is the winner of four Emmy Awards for scripts and documentaries. She is also First Prize winner in the 2020 Lascaux Poetry Contest. Her films and videos are shown internationally in museums, conferences, and on US Public Television. Now in her 70s, she has begun to publish the poetry she has been writing all her life (*Tipton Poetry Journal, Writers' Circle, London Reader,* and many others including various anthologies.) She writes poetry in the belief that only art can provide the clarity, compassion, and insight that is needed in the world.

Meniscus of Warmth and Silence
Elya Braden

The dark sea near my home
refuses to hold my name
in her mouth. Her language
bound in the hard consonants of
salt and north. I pace her hot
borders, outside the reach
of her greedy gulping tide, stare
at her as through a glass wall,
tempted and barred.

My spirit returns to me
in water. She larks with a pod
of dolphins, a hundred-year
wandering of sea turtles, a neon
spectacle of tiny fishes flashing
their bright markings in a saline
game of hide and seek in coral
reefs sheltered in a cove
south of Kona.

She plunges into the cliff-face
depths off the coast of a Balinese
island whose name has long since
skipped off my tongue. She
gawps in the shivered silence
of below, in the shifting shadow,
the bubbled breath, the flick and thrust
of flippers wedding me to all that glides
beneath the surface.

At night, I sink into the lavender
and eucalyptus waters
of my soaking tub, porcelain
bowl of memory, containing
every footprint on every beach
I've ever gamboled. The washcloth's
drift recalls the tug of kelp around
my ankles while the sponge's
bleached honeycomb floats
under shifting icebergs of bubbles,
all *hiss* and *pop*, scribing ephemeral
faces, animals and continents across
a meniscus of warmth
and silence.

Elya Braden is a writer and mixed-media artist living in Ventura County, California, and is Assistant Editor of *Gyroscope Review*. Her chapbook, *Open The Fist*, was released in 2020. Her second chapbook, *The Sight of Invisible Longing*, was a semi-finalist in Finishing Line Press's New Women's Voices Competition and will be published in 2023. Her work has been published in *Calyx, Prometheus Dreaming, Rattle Poets Respond, Sequestrum, Sheila-Na-Gig Online, The Coachella Review* and elsewhere. Her poems have been nominated for a Pushcart Prize and have received several Best of the Net nominations. www.elyabraden.com.

The brain and heart
Uma Kurt

I lean, watching you sip your gourmet wine
Twisting your skinny, little legs through summer sand
It is barbaric, the smile you carry
A reluctant feeling twists my chest
Carry on, don't allow me to interrupt
This pleasant vacation you appear to be taking
Let him take over, you are seamlessly occupied
He perfects madness, but don't let it reason with you
As of now, I am led by emotions, no longer conscious

Uma Kurt is a high school student in Sarajevo, Bosnia

Unforgettable
Roy Bentley

Prayer is one big bonfire of hope, so I light a fire
and pray. Send smoke in no particular direction since

it says, in the holy books I've read, you're everywhere.
You're in the bear in flames on a burning riverbank,

in the white-tailed doe forcefully leading a fawn
past one more sunlight-colored conflagration

in California or Oregon, a world away from Ohio,
where the wreck of our lives plays out differently.

Isn't that God in the earpiece of the first responder?
Nat King Cole saying we're unforgettable, in song,

more of that than anything else? And if that's true,
who then blesses these struggles to keep breathing?

I read how defense forces in Ukraine in trenches
hunker down and rest and rearm. In their eyes

today, smoke arabesques from the gun barrel
withdrawing from the ripped-up curtain and

a baker's boy from Kyiv is sniper-shot. Dead,
he sat down into himself as opposed to falling.

I like to think he collapsed with ravens in his
eyes as, neighboring, party-balloons flew up

and brave locals choreographed a Michael
Jackson song—something from *Thriller*.

Roy Bentley lives in Ohio and is the author of *Walking with Eve in the Loved City*, chosen by Billy Collins as finalist for the Miller Williams poetry prize; *Starlight Taxi*, winner of the Blue Lynx Poetry Prize; *The Trouble with a Short Horse in Montana*, chosen by John Gallaher as winner of the White Pine Poetry Prize; as well as *My Mother's Red Ford: New & Selected Poems 1986 – 2020* published by Lost Horse Press. Poems have appeared in *North American Review, The Southern Review, Rattle, Shenandoah, New Ohio Review,* and *Prairie Schooner* among others. His latest is *Beautiful Plenty* (Main Street Rag, 2021).

Emergence

Stacy Savage

Hundreds of black flowing tears
down my cheeks,
Soaking my pillow
With the rain inside.
Long sleeves in summer
To hide shades of black and blue.
Living on diet pills
With the words "you're fat"
burned into my brain.
I felt like a caterpillar
Squirming to break free
From a web of
Deceit and pain,
But I escaped
And broke the threads
Of confinement.
I emerged from a cocoon
And found a beautiful flower
That supported me
and helped me spread my wings
And take flight
to a wonderful life of new beginnings
with peace, confidence,
and the nectar
of love.

Stacy Savage has published several anthologies that benefited multiple charities. Her work has been published in numerous publications, including *Birds and Blooms, Ideals,* and *Asian Geographic.* She was a judge twice in the former Best Books of Indiana competition that was held by the Indiana State Library. She's currently working on a tree project that she expects to be published in Spring 2022.

First Star

Lois Marie Harrod

All matter created in the Big Bang was mostly hydrogen (75%) and helium (25). The first stars evolved without the heavier elements, were huge and disappeared quickly.

Some days I want to go back
to my beginning, back to my first star,

the ones astronomers are searching for,
my first glance after the Big Bang,

glint uncontaminated by lithium,
spark without carbon or magnesium or calcium,

star unstained by iron, oh, how simple I was—
first sun before my sun, before the stars,

before the galaxies and all their wars,
first star that flashed and was dark, a prophecy,

the star that made me, that wink in the bucket of stars,
flash, sputter, shimmer, trace, spark, splinter

wick flicking as the flame
before earth began its slow spinning

around my familiar, the sun, huge
this morning on the horizon,

a great wound in the firmament.
How it seems to ache—

haven't I always made things bigger than they seem?—
and now these patches of light flickering on the birch,

what did I do my first three days,
was it this? Matter forgets almost everything—

first star, second, fifth, generations of light,
there was I, every sun as old as the first, every particle,

13.8 billion years, the clock I carry in my wrist.

Lois Marie Harrod's *Spat* was published in June 2021. Her 17th collection *Woman* won the 2020 Blue Lyra Prize. *Nightmares of the Minor Poet* appeared in June 2016 (Five Oaks); her chapbook *And She Took the Heart*, in January 2016; *Fragments from the Biography of Nemeis and How Marlene Mae Longs for Truth* (Dancing Girl Press) appeared in 2013. A Dodge poet, she lives in New Jersey and is published in literary journals and online ezines from *American Poetry Review* to *Zone 3*. Online link: www.loismarieharrod.org

Narration
Michael Keshigian

The other men,
in their ostentatious outfits,
attempted to entice her
with idle bravado,
drinks or a dance.
He watched
as they huddled around her,
competing for her attention
with intense glances
which said much more than hello.
He bid his time in a corner,
where smoke filled air
stained his eyes.
Far from the embattled contestants.
he wrote on a pad,
describing her voice and beauty,
thoughts he knew
he would one day read to her
when they were perfected
and courage allowed him
to rouse her from the customary
into the extraordinary ardor
of his verse.
He would be the different one,
the flushed eccentric
with common clothes
and a black notebook,
thick with words
she had never heard before.
He would be the charming misfit
who, in a warm summer breeze,
on the edge of night,
will capture her affection
with a narrative
it took so many nights to contrive.

Hidden Amid the Stars
Michael Keshigian

It wasn't easy,
living with him,
his moody character
and need for privacy,
the all night creative fits
while she tried to sleep.
She interrupted him
in the middle of a thousand poems
for household information,
invaded his reverie
on the blue hill mountain pass
as the view sung an ode
in his brain,
even conquered his triumph
over an elusive phrase
when she yelled up
for dinner.
But he clung to her,
his raft on the white water swirls,
stability upon the rumbling current
of perpetual thought.
Often, he floated alone,
submerged in foam,
gagging for the tangible
and she would grxab a handful of hair,
yank his heavy head up.
They stumbled through silence,
blundered through varied perspectives,
yet when the river calmed,
they studied the stars
to find out exactly
where they were going.

Michael Keshigian had his fourteenth poetry collection, *What To Do With Intangibles*, recently released in January, 2020 by Cyberwit.net. He has been published in numerous national and international journals and has appeared as feature writer in twenty publications with 7 Pushcart Prize and 2 Best Of The Net nominations. (michaelkeshigian.com)

Dear Death,

Paul Lojeski

I spotted you the other day on
top of the hill across the street
from me, in that wind and snow
but I saw you, friend, and that
look of expectation crossing
those shiny red eyes but you
took off, busy elsewhere in
millions of places, taking your
new friends down into your
sunken bone yards full of
wretched treasures but I know
you'll return, getting closer
with each visit because you're
not far off from claiming me,
as well. This sad old flesh ready
for the taking. I don't mind,
so come along any time, bring it.

All the Best,

Paul

Paul Lojeski was born and raised in Lakewood, Ohio. He attended Oberlin College. His poetry has appeared online and in print. He lives in Port Jefferson, New York.

Review: My Body the Guitar by Karla Linn Merrifield
Reviewed by Barry Harris

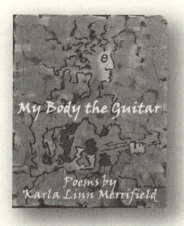

Title: My Body the Guitar

Author: Karla Linn Merrifield

Year: 2021

Publisher: Before Your Quiet Eyes Publications

Once upon a time, when Karla Linn Merrifield was ten years old, a guitar came into her life. But it belonged to her 15 year-old brother. He was a natural guitarist while she describes herself as "shackled to the old upright piano in the basement." Fifty years later, she began writing this book and decided she should learn how to play the guitar to better understand the mastery of the guitar gods who now populate the subjects of the third and final section of *My Body the Guitar*. So, she bought a Martin 000GT16.

My Body the Guitar is arranged, as if itself a triptych, in three sections. The first section, titled *Mere Mortal*, describes, documents, and celebrates the poet's struggle (or obsession) with learning to play guitar — from building finger callouses, through learning chords and tabulature and growing into a full-blown love affair with her guitars. The next section, *Local Heroes*, explores poetically those memories and stories of a life accompanied mostly by music. In the third section, *Mighty Gods*, Merrifield reveals to us her take on the mighty guitar gods of our time — now that she has travelled her own guitar journey to approach their heights.

Where to begin? The introduction says that the answer to how she coneived of the book is in the poem "Serendipitous Liaison." That's probably a good place.

> *I carried the ovum of the idea*
> *with me to your home*
> *despite our only intentions: do*
> *weed, wine, the deed*
>
> *But then you whipped out*
> *your 2010 Custom Gibson Les Paul,*
> *slapped it in my bare lap,*
> *heavy and warm and solid.*
>
> *I stroked the length of him,*
> *you pointing out during my fondling,*
> > *That's the nut; that's the bridge;*
> > *those the triple pickups.*

The idea is born. The poet becomes a guitarist. Soon, she has purchased her own Martin 000GT16, as revealed to us in "Metamorphical Metamorphosis."

> *Voilà! guitar gigolo, Boner by name.*
> *Bingo! Martin triple-ought Gt16*
> *bought, paid for, hefted off*
> *to have and to hold I dreamed*
> *in some quasi-disciplined fashion:*
> *but daily his mahogany wood-warm*
> *resonates with my warm-blooded woman body.*

What follows next are The Boner Etudes, several dozen short poems chronicling the experience of teaching oneself to play the guitar, who Merrifield has named Boner. One of my favorites:

> **Etude 8-3: Day 3**
> *Come to Mama:*
> *Does the D chord make you hard*
> *cuz it's so hard for me to do*

Those who are already musically inclined will appreciate Merrifield's detailed delving into musicology. But for those of us who have never before wondered how to play a D thirteen flat with five flat nine, the poet assures us that it is indeed a painful jazz chord.

It should be noted that a few months into the author's journey into self-teaching herself guitar, she (as did all of us) wandered into the wilderness of COVID-19.

> *Étude 4-14: Coronavirus Cameo, Day 30*
>
> *I ask my guitar*
> *the only warmed thing*
> *I have to hold onto now*
> *will I ever make love again*
>
> *the longer we play today*
> *the warmer I become*
> *able to tease from him*
> *his answer in diminished 7ths*

The poem *Heaven?* appears to have been written in anticipation of acquiring a new electric guitar (an AVA Guitars Bloody Pearl model), which Merrifield names Bhalz. It is a quite clever allusion to Led Zeppelin's classic *Stairway to Heaven*.

> *Thou preparest the stairway to heaven*
> *in the presence of coronavirus:*
>
> *thou shall anointest my fingers with impeccable frets;*
> *my lyrics shall runneth over.*
>
> *Surely humming pipers calling will join me*
> *all the remaining days of my life:*
>
> *and I shall dwell in custom-comfort whatever,*
> *listening to thee and me forever.*

The third and final section ("Mighty Gods") of Karla Linn Merrifield's *My Body the Guitar* is a compendium of poetic tributes to the particular guitar gods in her musical pantheon. Most are generally known, others are obvious, and a few worth researching to learn a thing or two about them.

An average reader, if unmusical, may find some elements of Merrifield's poetry obscure. But this book should not be read as a poetical technical manual on how to play chords. The final stanza of "Tanka Triptych: Joni" ends with:

> Learn A7sus-
> tained, because we are stardust;
> we are golden chords.
> and your A7sus, its 3rd
> omitted, strums memory.

A reader may also find themselves enticed, envying the poet who encompasses both worlds of music and poetry. If you have lived through the majority of a century with rock music in the background – or just sampled the distant past of your elders on Spotify lists – you can also begin to understand that this book is an intimate confessional (or a Leonard Cohen "holy Halleujah') celebrating the relationship of music and spirit, or the body of a guitar and the body of a woman.

Karla Linn Merrifield has had 1000+ poems appear in dozens of journals and anthologies. She has 14 books to her credit. Following her 2018 *Psyche's Scroll* (Poetry Box Select) is the 2019 full-length book *Athabaskan Fractal: Poems of the Far North* from Cirque Press. Her newest poetry collection, *My Body the Guitar*, inspired by famous guitarists and their guitars, was published in December 2021 by Before Your Quiet Eyes Publications Holograph Series (Rochester, New York). Karla now lives in Florida.

Barry Harris is editor of the *Tipton Poetry Journal* and four anthologies by Brick Street Poetry. He has published one poetry collection, *Something At The Center*.

Married and father of two grown sons, Barry lives in Brownsburg, Indiana and is retired from Eli Lilly and Company.

His poetry has appeared in *Kentucky Review, Valparaiso Poetry Review, Grey Sparrow, Silk Road Review, Saint Ann's Review, North Dakota Quarterly, Boston Literary Magazine, Night Train, Silver Birch Press, Flying Island, Awaken Consciousness, Writers' Bloc, Red-Headed Stepchild* and *Laureate: The Literary Journal of Arts for Lawrence*.

He graduated a long time ago with a major in English from Ball State University.

Review: Catena Poetica: An International Collaboration
Reviewed by Dan Carpenter

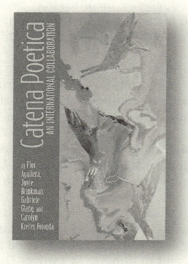

Title: <u>Catena Poetica: An International Collaboration</u>

Authors: Flor Aguilera, Joyce Brinkman, Gabriele Glang, Carolyn Kreiter-Foronda

Year: 2022

Publisher: Finishing Line Press

What could be more congenially cosmopolitan than a five-course feast of the senses?

Four poets representing three nations submit what they proclaim as an original answer in the form of a new chapbook of collaborative work that challenges each of them to up the enticement and elevate the conversation.

Catena Poetica brings together Flor Aguilera of Mexico, German-American Gabriele Glang, former Virginia poet laureate Carolyn Kreiter-Foronda and former Indiana poet laureate Joyce Brinkman in the joint production of five groupings of interrelated poems under headings that serve as a kind of sensory Esperanza: *Color, Spice, Music, Water, Clouds*.

The titles are metaphorical, mythological, historical, philosophical, spiritual. But first and always, they mean what they say. *Music* is an onomatopoetic extravaganza of pounding drums, mothers' hums, rattling seeds and "people / breathing long before cathedral organs / pumped air through golden pipes." *Spice* with its verbal bazaar of "sweet paprika" and "fragrant waves of clove" and "parsley, rosemary / and thyme" beckons the (older?) reader to bring the page or screen up close for a whiff à la the mimeograph sheets of school days. *Clouds* invites us to

> *Contemplate the mammatus*
> *clouds clotting a creamy sky—*
> *heavy-breasted auguries*
> *of Indian Summer's end.*

Delightful as the conveyance to our facial faculties may be, however, the poets' ambitions go much farther. The senses in each category are multisensory, if you will; given to imagery and capabilities interwoven with one another.

Not only are we warmed by the sun's light in *Color*; we can taste the sun itself. Our forbears in ancient times "wondered who / carried the sun." In *Water*, the moon's light will be "mangled" by the sea's surface, while "Waves and mermaids will call out" to a beloved human who ignores their serenade.

Sun worshippers, mermaids. Mythology is a bright essential thread followed and extended throughout in keeping with the *renku* tradition of collaborative verse that Aguilera in particular sought to give a contemporary revival.

The highly prescriptive format calls for three of the poets to compose a narrative for each section, with the first poet to introduce the theme in two tercets followed by a couplet, to broadly address the theme, to install a mythological figure or god, and to italicize key words that must be used in subsequent poets' narratives.

As these talented contributors demonstrate, the formula allows plenty of latitude for them to rhapsodize, improvise and infuse with flavorings from their respective cultures and far beyond.

From *Color*:

> *Let us praise chaos, maligned precursor*
> *of transitions. A ragged mizzle veils*
> *barely greening meadows. March's Ides rack*
> *the eaves, silencing birdsong. Wild winds roar*
> *in bone-bare branches. Rain clouds surge, engorged*
> *with the salty taste of ambivalence:*
> *that yearning to be traveling – Fernweh –*
> *or buried in the sofa all day long.*

From *Spice*:

> *Fortunate the fowl, the pigs of the poor.*
> *With masters of meager means, unable*
> *to sacrifice such precious possessions,*
> *livestock likenesses took their place*
> *on ghost-white Springerles. Cookies*
> *scented with sweet, aromatic anise oil.*
> *An infused Christmas treat instead of*
> *meat to amuse a small German girl.*
>
> *Fair is beautiful and upright.*
> *Fair is lightness and warm weather.*
> *In this land it is just the right amount.*
> *Tortilla maker creates maize from stone.*
> *Open hand a perfect measuring cup,*
> *she adds the hint of paprika, spice, and sauce.*
> *This dish requires generosity in plating,*
> *a sharp tongue to withstand all the color and heat.*

Sometimes, the tastes we're offered can be anything but savory. From *Water*, for example:

> *A young boy's gunshots sail*
> *across a shallow creek,*
> *rattle a sliding glass door,*
> *the elderly victims, sprawled*
> *on the floor. The rain, persistent,*
> *pounds earth, its path*
> *foreboding in a climate*
> *rife with firearms.*
>
> *Persistent bloodstream,*
> *difficult to clean up, dry, erase on map.*

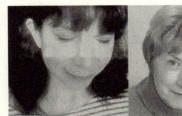

Flor Aguilera Kreiter-Foronda   Joyce Brinkman   Gabriele Glang   Carolyn

Catena Poetica follows the 2014 publication of *Seasons of Sharing* (Leapfrog Press), a collaborative book of modified kasen renku verse by Aguilera, Brinkman, Kreiter-Foronda and writers from Japan, Germany and France. Among their host of credentials and honors, **Flor Aguilera** is the author of six books, **Carolyn Kreiter-Foronda** has published nine books and co-edited three poetry anthologies, **Gabriele Glang** is a widely published bilingual writer as well as a teacher and film translator, and **Joyce Brinkman** is instrumental in Brick Street Poetry Inc.'s many Indiana outreach programs and the author of *Elizabeth Barrett Browning Illuminated by the Message*.

Dan Carpenter is the author of two collections of poetry and two books of non-fiction. He has contributed poems and stories to many journals and anthologies. He blogs at dancarpenterpoet.wordpress.com.

Editor

Barry Harris is editor of the *Tipton Poetry Journal* and four anthologies by Brick Street Poetry: *Mapping the Muse: A Bicentennial Look at Indiana Poetry; Words and Other Wild Things* and *Cowboys & Cocktails:Poems from the True Grit Saloon*, and *Reflections on Little Eagle Creek*. He has published one poetry collection, *Something At The Center*.

Married and father of two grown sons, Barry lives in Brownsburg, Indiana and is retired from Eli Lilly and Company.

His poetry has appeared in *Kentucky Review, Valparaiso Poetry Review, Grey Sparrow, Silk Road Review, Saint Ann's Review, North Dakota Quarterly, Boston Literary Magazine, Night Train, Silver Birch Press, Flying Island, Awaken Consciousness, Writers' Bloc, Red-Headed Stepchild* and *Laureate: The Literary Journal of Arts for Lawrence*. One of his poems was on display at the National Museum of Sport and another is painted on a barn in Boone County, Indiana as part of Brick Street Poetry's Word Hunger public art project. His poems are also included in these anthologies: *From the Edge of the Prairie; Motif 3: All the Livelong Day;* and *Twin Muses: Art and Poetry*.

He graduated a long time ago with a major in English from Ball State University.

Contributor Biographies

Duane Anderson currently lives in La Vista, Nebraska, and volunteers with a non-profit organization as a Donor Ambassador on their blood drives. He has had poems published in *The Pangolin Review, Fine Lines, The Sea Letter, Cholla Needles, Tipton Poetry Journal, Adelaide Literary Magazine* and several other publications.

Ayomide Bayowa is the (2021-24) poet laureate of Mississauga, Ontario, Canada. He became the first place in the 2020 July Open Drawer Poetry Contest, the June/ July 2021 Edition of the Bi-monthly Brigitte Poirson Poetry Contest (BPPC). He was a top-ten gold entrant of the 9th Open Eurasian Literary Festival, U.K, and a semi-finalist of the 2021 Cave Canem Poetry Prize. He has appeared in a long list of literary magazines, some of which are *Barren Magazine, Agbowó, Guesthouse-Lit, Stone of Madness Press*. He currently reads poetry for *Adroit Journal*.

Joe Benevento's poems, stories, essays and reviews have appeared in close to 300 places, including: *Poets & Writers, I-70 Review* and *Bilingual Review*. He is the author of fourteen books of poetry and fiction, including: *Expecting Songbirds: Selected Poems, 1983-2015*. He teaches creative writing and American literature at Truman State University in Kirksville, Missouri. and is the poetry editor for the *Green Hills Literary Lantern*.

Roy Bentley lives in Ohio and is the author of *Walking with Eve in the Loved City*, chosen by Billy Collins as finalist for the Miller Williams poetry prize; *Starlight Taxi*, winner of the Blue Lynx Poetry Prize; *The Trouble with a Short Horse in Montana*, chosen by John Gallaher as winner of the White Pine Poetry Prize; as well as *My Mother's Red Ford: New & Selected Poems 1986 – 2020* published by Lost Horse Press. Poems have appeared in *North American Review, The Southern Review, Rattle, Shenandoah, New Ohio Review,* and *Prairie Schooner* among others. His latest is *Beautiful Plenty* (Main Street Rag, 2021).

Elena Botts has lived many places in the northeast and abroad, currently in New York state. Her poems have been published in over a hundred literary magazines, and she is the winner of four poetry contests and has had many books published. Her visual artwork has won numerous awards and has been exhibited in various galleries. Elena has also collaborated on, released and installed sound and moving image artwork, as well as multimedia and conceptual art, and formed a multimedia collective for this purpose, while pursuing graduate school, human rights, and arts projects.

Elya Braden is a writer and mixed-media artist living in Ventura County, California, and is Assistant Editor of *Gyroscope Review*. Her chapbook, *Open The Fist*, was released in 2020. Her second chapbook, *The Sight of Invisible Longing*, was a semi-finalist in Finishing Line Press's New Women's Voices Competition and will be published in 2023. Her work has been published in *Calyx, Prometheus Dreaming, Rattle Poets Respond, Sequestrum, Sheila-Na-Gig Online, The Coachella Review* and elsewhere. Her poems have been nominated for a Pushcart Prize and have received several Best of the Net nominations. www.elyabraden.com.

Matthew Brennan's poems have appeared in *Poetry Salzburg, Concho River Review, Valparaiso Poetry Review, THINK, Paterson Literary Review, Tipton Poetry Journal,* and others. His most recent book is *Snow in New York: New and Selected Poems* (2021). He taught for 32 years at Indiana State University and now lives in Columbus, Ohio.

Luanne Castle's *Kin Types* (Finishing Line Press), a chapbook of poetry and flash nonfiction, was a finalist for the Eric Hoffer Award. Her first collection of poetry, *Doll God*, winner of the New Mexico-Arizona Book Award for Poetry, was published by Aldrich Press. Luanne has been a Fellow at the Center for Ideas and Society at the University of California, Riverside. She studied English and Creative Writing at the University of California, Riverside (PhD); Western Michigan University (MFA); and Stanford University. Her Pushcart and Best of the Net-nominated poetry and prose have appeared in *Copper Nickel, American Journal of Poetry, Pleiades, River Teeth, TAB, Verse Daily, Glass: A Journal of Poetry, Saranac Review, Grist,* and other journals. An avid blogger, she can be found at luannecastle.com. She lives in Arizona, where she shares land with a bobcat.

Yuan Changming hails with Allen Yuan from poetrypacific.blogspot.ca. Credits include 12 Pushcart nominations & chapbooks (most recently *Limerence*) besides appearances in *Best of the Best Canadian Poetry* (2008-17) & *Best New Poems Online*, among more than 1900 others. Yuan served on the jury, and was nominated, for Canada's National Magazine Awards (poetry category) and lives in Vancouver.

Elizabeth Crowell grew up in northern New Jersey and has a B.A. from Smith College in English Literature and an M.F.A. in Creative Writing/Poetry from Columbia University. She taught college and high school English for many years and lives outside of Boston with her wife and teenage children.

After 34 years with Eli Lilly and Company, **Brendan Crowley** set up his own consulting and executive coaching business, Brendan Crowley Advisors LLC. He helps executives grow in their roles and careers. Brendan is originally from Ireland and lives with his wife Rosaleen in Zionsville, Indiana. He has a passion for photography and loves taking photographs of his home country, Ireland, and here in Indiana.

Jill Evans, aka: Jill Evans Petzall, makes documentary films, media art installations, writes poetry, and teaches about social justice from a female perspective. She lives in St. Louis, Missouri. Her work is fueled by a graduate degree in Philosophy and her faith in the power of storytelling. She is the winner of four Emmy Awards for scripts and documentaries. She is also First Prize winner in the 2020 Lascaux Poetry Contest. Her films and videos are shown internationally in museums, conferences, and on US Public Television. Now in her 70s, she has begun to publish the poetry she has been writing all her life (*Tipton Poetry Journal, Writers' Circle, London Reader,* and many others including various anthologies.) She writes poetry in the belief that only art can provide the clarity, compassion, and insight that is needed in the world.

Marjie Giffin is a Midwestern writer who has authored four regional histories and whose poetry has appeared in *Snapdragon, Poetry Quarterly, Flying Island, The Kurt Vonnegut Literary Journal, Saint Katherine Review, Northwest Indiana Literary Journal, Blue Heron Review, Tipton Poetry Journal, Agape Review* and the anthologies *The Lives We Have Live(d)* and *What Was and What Will Be, Leave them Something,* and *Reflections on Little Eagle Creek.* Her work was recently featured online by the Heartland Society of Women Writers and her first chapbook, *Touring,* was published in 2021. She lives in Indianapolis and is active in the Indiana Writers' Center and has taught both college writing and gifted education.

William Greenway's 13th collection, As Long As We're Here, is forthcoming from FutureCycle Press. His *Selected Poems* was the Poetry Book of the Year Award winner from FutureCycle Press, and his tenth collection, *Everywhere at Once,* won the Poetry Book of the Year Award from the Ohio Library Association, as did his eighth collection *Ascending Order*. Publications include *Poetry, American Poetry Review, Southern Review, Missouri Review, Georgia Review, Southern Poetry Review, Prairie Schooner, Poetry Northwest,* and *Shenandoah*. Greenway is Distinguished Professor of English Emeritus at Youngstown State University, and now lives in Ephrata, Pennsylvania.

John Grey is an Australian poet, US resident, recently published in the *New World Writing, Dalhousie Review and Blood And Thunder*. Work upcoming in *Hollins Critic, Redactions and California Quarterly*. John lives in Rhode Island.

Lois Marie Harrod's *Spat* was published in June 2021. Her 17th collection *Woman* won the 2020 Blue Lyra Prize. *Nightmares of the Minor Poet* appeared in June 2016 (Five Oaks); her chapbook *And She Took the Heart*, in January 2016; *Fragments from the Biography of Nemeis and How Marlene Mae Longs for Truth* (Dancing Girl Press) appeared in 2013. A Dodge poet, she lives in New Jersey and is published in literary journals and online ezines from *American Poetry Review* to *Zone 3*. Online link: www.loismarieharrod.org

Michael Keshigian had his fourteenth poetry collection, *What To Do With Intangibles*, recently released in January, 2020 by Cyberwit.net. He has been published in numerous national and international journals and has appeared as feature writer in twenty publications with 7 Pushcart Prize and 2 Best Of The Net nominations. (michaelkeshigian.com)

Uma Kurt is a high school student in Sarajevo, Bosnia

Bruce Levine has spent his life as a writer of fiction and poetry and as a music and theatre professional. A 2019 Pushcart Prize Poetry nominee, a 2021 Spillwords Press Awards winner, the Featured Writer in WestWard Quarterly Summer 2021 and his bio is featured in *Who's Who of Emerging Writers 2020*. Bruce has over three hundred works published on over twenty-five on-line journals including *Ariel Chart, Spillwords, The Drabble*; in over seventy print books including *Poetry Quarterly, Haiku Journal, Tipton Poetry Journal; Halcyon Days and Founder's Favourites* (on-line and print) and his shows have been produced in New York and around the country. His work is dedicated to the loving memory of his late wife, Lydia Franklin. A native Manhattanite, Bruce now lives and writes in Maine. Visit him at www.brucelevine.com

Paul Lojeski was born and raised in Lakewood, Ohio. He attended Oberlin College. His poetry has appeared online and in print. He lives in Port Jefferson, New York.

Doris Lynch has recent work in *Flying Island, Failed Haiku, Contemporary Haibun Online,* and *Drifting Sands Haibun*. She has lived in places as varied as arctic Alaska, Yogyakarta, Indonesia, New Orleans, Berkeley, and for the last twenty-some years in Bloomington, Indiana.

Jennifer L. McClellan is an Evansville, Indiana based poet whose poems have been published in the *Tipton Poetry Journal, Flying Island, Stirring: A Literary Collection, The Green Hills Literary Lantern* as well as an upcoming issue of *The The Round Table Literary Journal*.

Karla Linn Merrifield has had 1000+ poems appear in dozens of journals and anthologies. She has 14 books to her credit. Following her 2018 *Psyche's Scroll* (Poetry Box Select) is the 2019 full-length book *Athabaskan Fractal: Poems of the Far North* from Cirque Press. Her newest poetry collection, *My Body the Guitar*, inspired by famous guitarists and their guitars, was published in December 2021 by Before Your Quiet Eyes Publications Holograph Series (Rochester, New York). Karla now lives in Florida.

Maria S. Picone/수영 is a Korean American adoptee who won *Cream City Review's* 2020 Summer Poetry Prize. She has been published in *Tahoma Literary Review, The Seventh Wave, Fractured Lit* and more including *Best Small Fictions 2021*. Her work has been supported by *Lighthouse Writers Workshop, GrubStreet, Kenyon Review*, and *Tin House*. She is a 2022 Palm Beach Poetry Festival Kundiman Fellow and Chestnut Review's managing editor. She lives in South Carolina and is also the poetry editor at *Hanok Review* and associate editor at *Uncharted Mag*. Her work explores hybridity, identity, languages, and pop culture. Her website is mariaspicone.com, Twitter @mspicone.

Tom Raithel grew up in Milwaukee, Wisconsin and has worked as a journalist at several newspapers in the Midwest. Recently from Evansville, Indiana, today, he lives in Cleveland, Ohio with his wife, Theresa. His poems have appeared in *The Southern Review, The Comstock Review, Nimrod, Midwest Quarterly, Atlanta Review,* and other journals. Finishing Line Press has published his chapbook, *Dark Leaves, Strange Light*.

Stacy Savage lives in Yorktown, Indiana, and has published several anthologies that benefited multiple charities. Her work has been published in numerous publications, including *Birds and Blooms, Ideals,* and *Asian Geographic*. She was a judge twice in the former Best Books of Indiana competition that was held by the Indiana State Library. She's currently working on a tree project that she expects to be published in Spring 2022.

Claire Scott is an award winning poet in Oakland, California who has received multiple Pushcart Prize nominations. Her work has been accepted by the *Atlanta Review, Bellevue Literary Review, New Ohio Review, Enizagam* and *Healing Muse* among others. Claire is the author of *Waiting to be Called* and *Until I Couldn't*. She is the co-author of *Unfolding in Light: A Sisters' Journey in Photography and Poetry*.

Maureen Sherbondy has been published in *Calyx, European Judaism, The Oakland Review, Prelude,* and other journals. Her poetry books include *Eulogy for an Imperfect Man, Beyond Fairy Tales, The Art of Departure*, and six chapbooks. *Dancing with Dali* was published by FutureCycle Press in 2020. *Lines in Opposition* will be published by Unsolicited Press in 2022. She has also published a short story collection, *The Slow Vanishing*. Maureen teaches at Alamance Community College and lives in Durham, North Carolina, with her husband Barry Peters and her cat Lola.

Saurabh Sinha is a physician in Philadelphia writing poetry about everyday life, with subjects ranging from profound moments with patients to the new role of fatherhood to simply walking his dog.

Ian C. Smith's work has been published in *Antipodes, BBC Radio 4 Sounds,The Dalhousie Review, Griffith Review, San Pedro River Review , Southword, The Stony Thursday Book, & Two Thirds North*. His seventh book is *wonder sadness madness joy*, Ginninderra (Port Adelaide). He writes in the Gippsland Lakes area of Victoria, Australia and on Flinders Island.

VA Smith lives in Philadelphia and has published poetry in dozens of literary journals and anthologies, among them *Blue Lake Review, Ginosko Literary Journal, MacQueen's*

Quinterly, Mobius, Quartet, The Southern Review, Verdad, Third Wednesday, Oyster River Pages, and forthcoming in *Evening Street Review* and *West Trade Review,* Her book *Biking Through the Stone Age* will be published by Kelsay Books in Spring 2022. Currently, she's finishing a collection titled *America's Daughters & Other Poems* and ignoring her Peleton.

Jeanine Stevens is the author of *Inheritor and Limberlost* (Future Cycle Press), and *Sailing on Milkweed* (Cherry Grove Collections). She is winner of the MacGuffin Poet Hunt and The Ekphrasis Prize. Gertrude Sitting: Portraits of Women, won the 2020 Chapbook Prize from Heartland Review Press. Jeanine recently received her seventh Pushcart Nomination. She studied poetry at U.C. Davis and Community of Writers, Olympic Valley and is Faculty Emerita at American River College.

Jeffrey S. Thompson was raised in Fargo, North Dakota, and educated at the University of Iowa and Cornell Law School. He lives and works in Phoenix, Arizona. At Iowa he participated in undergraduate poetry workshops and had a couple poems published in small journals. He pursued a career in public interest law, but recently decided to start sharing his work again. Thompson was named a finalist for the 2021 *Iowa Review Poetry* Award, and has been published or accepted at *Neologism Poetry Journal, North Dakota Quarterly, The Main Street Rag,* and *Passengers Journal.*

Victoria Twomey is a fine art illustrator and the author of several chapbooks, including *Autumn Music Box* and *The Feminine Voice*. She has appeared as a featured poet at various venues around Long Island, New York, including "First Fridays" at the Hecksher Museum of Art, The Poetry Barn, Barnes & Noble, The Pisces Cafe, Borders Books and local radio. Her poems have been published in several anthologies, in newspapers and on the Web. Her poem "Pieta" was nominated for a Pushcart Prize by *Long Island Sounds 2006: An Anthology of Poetry From Maspeth to Montauk and Beyond.*

David Vancil is retired from the faculty of Indiana State University. His work has appeared in small periodicals, critical reviews, and a few anthologies. As well, he is the author of four poetry collections. *War and Its Discontents*, a collection of military poems centered on family service and his own time in the U.S. Army, will be published by Angelina River Press sometime in 2022. He is at work on a collection of new and selected poems, which he hopes to publish no later than 2023. David lives in Terre Haute, Indiana, with his wife, three cats, and a dog.

Anne Whitehouse's recent poetry collection is *Outside from the Inside* (Dos Madres Press, 2020), and her recent chapbook is *Escaping Lee Miller* (Ethel Zine and Micro Press, 2021).. Anne is also the author of a novel, *Fall Love,* and she has been publishing a series of essays about Edgar Allan Poe. She lives in New York City and Columbia County, New York. www.annewhitehouse.com

Alessio Zanelli is an Italian poet who writes in English and whose work has appeared in over 200 literary journals from 16 countries. His fifth original collection, titled *The Secret Of Archery*, was published in 2019 by Greenwich Exchange Publishing (London). For more information please visit www.alessiozanelli.it.

Made in the USA
Coppell, TX
20 March 2022

75276212R00042